Betty Saw's
Teatime Treats

Asian Favourites to Make and Bake

Marshall Cavendish
Cuisine

The publisher wishes to thank Robinsons & Co and Java Enterprises Pte Ltd for the loan and use of their tableware.

First published as Asian High Tea Favourites © Times Books International 1979
Revised edition © Marshall Cavendish International (Asia) Private Limited 2004
This new edition with new recipes 2023

Photo Credits
All photos by Joshua Tan and Cedric Lim, except for the pages indicated below:
Betty Saw: 21, 23, 27, 39, 43, 51, 65, 69, 85, 97, 99, 105, 113, 115, 142
Adobe Stock: p 3, Cultura Creative; p 5 Iryna Melnyk; p 10 Sorapop;
p 60, Michelle; p 78, p 92, Pixel-Shot; p 110, FomaA; p 124, Bongkarn

Published by Marshall Cavendish Cuisine
An imprint of Marshall Cavendish International

A member of the
Times Publishing Group

Other Marshall Cavendish Offices:
Marshall Cavendish Corporation, 800 Westchester Ave, Suite N-641, Rye Brook, NY 10573, USA · Marshall Cavendish International (Thailand) Co Ltd, 253 Asoke, 16th Floor, Sukhumvit 21 Road, Klongtoey Nua, Wattana, Bangkok 10110, Thailand · Marshall Cavendish (Malaysia) Sdn Bhd, Times Subang, Lot 46, Subang Hi-Tech Industrial Park, Batu Tiga, 40000 Shah Alam, Selangor Darul Ehsan, Malaysia

Marshall Cavendish is a trademark of Times Publishing Limited

Printed in Singapore

Preface

For me, the very word "tea" carries with it fond memories of mouth-watering, scrumptious cakes, a blissful spread of cookies and luscious sweets, light and delicate pastries, fragrant golden loaves and buns, and delicious savouries.

I have enjoyed time and time again recipes which are now compiled in this book. They have gathered our families and friends to share many good times and celebrated occasions. They have been thoroughly enjoyed by all and I feel certain they will be enjoyed with equal enthusiasm and relish if you try them yourself. At the same time, you'll be passing on to your family, friends and guests, a store of memories of the taste of simple, good home baking and cooking in the relaxed atmosphere of your own home.

This book contains not only delectable familiar recipes, but also many exciting and imaginative creations, and fun ways to present and decorate your treats.

I have thoroughly enjoyed working through this book and I hope you'll make the most of it. I also hope that this book will prove to be an inspiring source in your own kitchen and that you'll find fun and pleasure in all your attempts.

Betty Saw

Contents

Kitchen Hints & Tips

- Preheat the oven to the specified temperature before baking.

- Use castor (superfine) sugar when a recipe calls for it because using coarser sugar can lead to inadequate creaming and the undissolved sugar granules can leave white specks on the cake's surface and ruin the look of your cake.

- Use large eggs for making cakes. Bring the eggs to room temperature before using because they produce a greater volume after beating than cold eggs of the same size.

- Eggs are classified according to size. Weighed in the shell, large eggs are generally 70–75 g; medium eggs are 60–65 g and small eggs are 55 g.

- When whisking eggs and sugar, beat at a high speed until the mixture is thick and pale.

- When beating egg whites for a meringue, ensure to cleanly separate the egg yolks and whites as the fat in the yolks can prevent the egg whites from beating up properly. Drops of egg yolk in egg whites can be easily removed using a piece of egg shell.

- When adding eggs to a creamed mixture, be careful not to do it too quickly as curdling will result. Should curdling occur, add a little flour from the recipe to the mixture to help it smoothen out.

- When folding in the flour in sponge cakes, do it quickly as air bubbles in the mixture will otherwise break. Air that has been beaten into the mixture and trapped in the form of bubbles is what gives sponge cakes their light and even texture.

- Scrape batter off the sides of the mixing bowl and mix it thoroughly with the rest of the bowl's contents. This will prevent uneven mixing which will lead to differently coloured streaks on the surface of the cake.

- When making self-raising flour at home, add 2 tsp baking powder to every 120 g plain (all-purpose) flour.

- When baking, avoid opening the oven door during the first 20 minutes as sudden rushes of cooler air can cause a cake to sink. Overheating an oven can also cause a cake to sink because the mixture has been forced to rise too quickly.

- When leaving a sponge cake out to cool, make sure that it is not placed in a spot that experiences rushes of cooler air as this will cause the cake to shrink and wrinkle. Undercooked sponge cakes can also shrink and wrinkle.

- Always check that a cake is thoroughly done before removing it from the oven. A good test is to insert a skewer into the centre of the cake, and if the skewer comes out clean, the cake is ready to be taken out of the oven.

- When serving sponge cakes, remember that they taste best on the day that they have been baked. Butter cakes keep well for several days in airtight containers, while gingerbread and fruit cakes improve in flavour over time.

- Always store cakes and biscuits in separate containers. When stored together, the biscuits will absorb the moisture from the cakes and become soft.

- Recipes in this book use fresh or reconstituted milk.

- Make sure that the water in the steamer is boiling before placing the items in to cook. Take the lid off the steamer carefully to avoid accidentedly scalding yourself.

CAKES

Pineapple Upside-Down Cake

Preparation time: 45 minutes   Baking time: 40–45 minutes   Oven setting: 175°C / 350°F

Ingredients

Pineapple rings	9
Red cherries	5, halved
Cold butter	250 g, cut into cubes
Castor (superfine) sugar	225 g
Large eggs	4
Vanilla essence	1 tsp
Self-raising flour	240 g
Pineapple juice	1–2 Tbsp

Pineapple Cream

Cold butter	250 g, cut into small cubes
Icing sugar	150 g, sifted
Vanilla essence	1 tsp
Cold evaporated milk	175 ml
Cold pineapple juice	2 Tbsp

Method

- Line a 22-cm square cake tin with greaseproof paper and grease well. Preheat oven to 175°C / 350°F.

- Arrange pineapple rings in three rows of three to cover base of tin. Place a cherry half in the centre of each ring.

- Cream butter and sugar until light and creamy. Add eggs one at a time. Add vanilla essence. Sift in half the flour and fold into mixture. Repeat with other half. Add pineapple juice to achieve soft, dropping consistency.

- Carefully spread batter over top of pineapple rings. Bake on centre shelf for 40–45 minutes or until a skewer inserted into the centre of cake comes out clean. Turn out and leave to cool on a wire rack.

- Prepare pineapple cream. Beat butter with sugar until light and creamy. Add vanilla essence. Beat in milk a little at a time. Beat in pineapple juice.

- Decorate cake as desired with pineapple cream.

Apple Cake

Preparation time: 20 minutes   Baking time: 45–60 minutes   Oven setting: 175°C / 350°F

Ingredients

Brown sugar	2–3 Tbsp
Plain (all-purpose) flour (A)	2 Tbsp, sifted
Ground cinnamon	2 tsp
Apples	4, peeled, cored and evenly sliced
Large eggs	4
Castor (superfine) sugar	225 g
Corn oil	250 ml
Vanilla essence	1 tsp
Salt	1 pinch
Cold water	150–180 ml
Plain (all-purpose) flour (B)	300 g
Baking powder	2 tsp

Method

- Line a 22-cm square cake tin with greased greaseproof paper. Preheat oven to 175°C / 350°F.

- Combine brown sugar, flour (A) and ground cinnamon in a bowl. Toss apple slices in bowl's contents. Set aside.

- Whisk eggs and sugar. Add corn oil, vanilla essence, salt and water. Sift in flour (B) and baking powder.

- Pour half the batter into prepared tin. Arrange apple slices on top. Spread remaining batter over apple slices to barely cover them. It does not matter if slices stick out.

- Bake for 45–60 minutes or until a skewer inserted into the centre of cake comes out clean. Turn out and leave to cool on a wire rack.

Orange Chiffon Cake

Preparation time: 20 minutes   Baking time: 75 minutes   Oven setting: 165°C / 325°F

Ingredients

Plain (all-purpose) flour	240 g
Baking powder	1 Tbsp
Castor (superfine) sugar	300 g
Corn oil	125 ml
Large eggs	7, yolks and whites separated
Orange rind	grated from 2 oranges
Orange juice or water	125 ml
Salt	$^1/_2$ tsp
Cream of tartar	$^1/_2$ tsp

Method

- Line base of a 27 x 9-cm tube pan with greaseproof paper and grease well. Preheat oven to 165°C / 325°F.

- Sift flour and baking powder together. Set aside.

- Beat sugar in corn oil. Add egg yolks. Beat until smooth. Add orange rind and juice or water. Fold in sifted ingredients quickly, together with salt. Set aside.

- Whisk cream of tartar and egg whites until stiff but not dry. Gently and gradually pour egg-yolk mixture over beaten egg whites. Mix evenly.

- Pour batter into prepared pan. Bake on lowest shelf for 75 minutes or until cake is springy to the touch.

Coconut Chiffon Cake

Preparation time: 30 minutes   Baking time: 75 minutes   Oven setting: 165°C / 325°F

Ingredients

Plain (all-purpose) flour	240 g
Baking powder	1 Tbsp
Large eggs	6, separated into yolks and whites
Sugar	280 g
Salt	$^1/_4$ tsp
Coconut milk	225 ml, squeezed from 1 grated coconut and sufficient water
Pandan juice	1 Tbsp, from pounding and squeezing pandan leaves
Green food colouring	a few drops
Cream of tartar	$^1/_2$ tsp
Corn oil	2 tsp

Method

- Grease a 25 x 9-cm tube pan. Preheat oven to 165°C / 325°F.

- Sift flour and baking powder together, twice. Set aside.

- Beat egg yolks, sugar and salt until white and creamy. Add coconut milk, pandan juice and food colouring. Sift in sifted ingredients. Fold in quickly but lightly.

- Whisk cream of tartar and egg whites until soft peaks form. Pour egg-yolk mixture over whisked egg whites. Mix lightly and evenly. Stir in corn oil.

- Pour batter into tube pan. Bake for 75 minutes.

- When done, invert onto a wire rack straightaway. Remove from tin after 5 minutes.

Cashew Nut Butter Cake

Preparation time: 20 minutes   Baking time: 40 minutes   Oven setting: 150°C / 300°F

Ingredients

Cake flour	240 g
Baking powder	2 tsp
Cold butter	280 g, cut into cubes
Castor (superfine) sugar	215 g
Vanilla essence	1 tsp
Large eggs	5
Milk	5 Tbsp
Natural yoghurt	3 Tbsp
Cashew nuts	120 g, chopped
Icing sugar	for dusting
Strawberries	to decorate

Method

- Line a 25-cm square cake tin with greaseproof paper and grease again. Preheat oven to 150°C / 300°F.

- Sift cake flour and baking powder together and set aside.

- Cream butter for 1 minute, then add castor sugar and vanilla essence. Beat until light and creamy.

- Add eggs, one at a time, beating well after addition. If mixture should curdle, beat in 90 g sifted flour in between addition of eggs.

- Fold in remaining flour. Stir in milk and yoghurt. Lastly, stir in cashew nuts.

- Bake for 40 minutes or until a skewer inserted into the centre of cake comes out clean.

- Leave cake to cool in tin before removing greaseproof paper.

- Place on a serving dish. Dust with icing sugar and decorate with strawberries before serving.

Hot Favourite Ginger Spice Cake

Preparation time: 20 minutes   Baking time: 60 minutes   Oven setting: 160°C / 320°F

Ingredients

Plain (all-purpose) flour	375 g
Bicarbonate of soda	2 tsp
Ground ginger	1 tsp
Butter	250 g, at room temperature
Dark brown muscovado sugar	250 g
Black treacle	250 g
Milk	300 ml
Large eggs	2
Glacè stem ginger	100 g, finely chopped

Icing

Icing sugar	5 Tbsp
Ginger syrup	3 Tbsp

Method

- Grease sides and line base of a 23-cm square baking tin. Preheat oven to 160°C / 320°F.

- Sift flour, bicarbonate of soda and ground ginger together. Set aside.

- Place butter, dark brown sugar and treacle into a saucepan and heat gently for about 5 minutes until butter and sugar have melted.

- Stir in milk. The mix should be warm to the touch. If not, leave to cool a little longer before beating in eggs.

- Mix chopped ginger and sifted ingredients together in a bowl of an electric mixer fitted with a beater. Add melted butter and sugar mixture and beat for 1 minute until batter is smooth.

- Pour batter into prepared baking tin. Bake for 1 hour until cake is risen and firm to the touch. A skewer inserted into the centre of cake should come out clean. Bake for another 5–10 minutes if needed, then test again.

- Remove from oven. Leave cake to cool in tin before turning out. Cover cake with cling wrap. This cake is best eaten 2–3 days after baking.

- To make icing, sift icing sugar into a bowl and add ginger syrup. Beat well until mixture is smooth and runny. Drizzle over cake. Cut into squares to serve.a wire rack to cool.

Rice Flour Sponge Cake

Preparation time: 15 minutes   Baking time: 45–47 minutes   Oven setting: 160°C / 320°F

Ingredients

Large eggs	5, yolks and whites separated
Milk	75 ml
Rice flour	140 g
Canola or other vegetable oil	55 ml
Vanilla essence	$1/2$ tsp
Castor (superfine) sugar	80 g
Cream of tartar	$1/4$ tsp

Method

- Prepare two baking tins. A 22.5-cm round cake tin and a pan large enough to hold it. Line the base of the 22.5 cm round cake pan with greaseproof paper. Leave sides unlined and ungreased.

- Preheat oven to 160°C / 320°F. Place cake tin in larger pan and fill pan with water until it comes halfway up the sides of cake tin. Remove and set cake tin aside.

- Place egg yolks and milk in a large mixing bowl. Using a handheld balloon whisk, stir mixture until well combined. Do not beat. Sift in rice flour and mix well. Stir in oil and vanilla essence. Set aside.

- In the bowl of an electric mixer fitted with a balloon whisk, beat egg whites and cream of tartar until frothy. Add sugar, one third at a time, and whisk until soft peaks form.

- Using a handheld balloon whisk, fold egg white mixture into egg yolk mixture one third at a time until well combined.

- Pour mixture from a height of about 30 cm into prepared cake tin. This is to remove any large air bubbles in the batter. Level surface.

- Place cake tin into pan of water in oven and bake for 35 minutes.

- Lower oven temperature to 140°C and bake for a further 10–12 minutes or until a skewer inserted into the centre of cake comes out clean.

- Carefully remove cake tin from oven and leave on a wire rack to cool for 10–15 minutes.

- To remove cake, pass a thin bladed knife around the sides and turn cake onto a wire rack. Remove greaseproof paper. Allow cake to cool completely before cutting.

Note:

If using a cake tin with a removeable base, wrap aluminum foil about halfway up the sides to prevent water from seeping in.

Indonesian Layer Cake (Kek Lapis)

Preparation time: 15 minutes　　Baking time: 60 minutes　　Oven setting: 175°C / 350°F

Ingredients

Butter	150 g, at room temperature
Eggs	7, yolks and whites separated
Sugar	150 g
Vanilla essence	1 tsp
Brandy	1 Tbsp
Plain (all-purpose) flour	90 g, sifted
Mixed spice	$^1/_4$ tsp, sifted

Method

- Grease base and sides of a 17-cm square cake tin. Line base with greaseproof paper and grease again. Preheat oven to 175°C / 350°F.

- Beat butter until creamy and set aside.

- Whisk eggs yolks, sugar and vanilla essence until creamy. Beat in butter and brandy. Stir in sifted ingredients. Set aside.

- Whisk eggs whites until just stiff. Pour egg-yolk mixture over beaten egg whites. Fold gently.

- Place prepared tin under preheated grill for 1 minute. Remove from grill and add a ladleful of batter. Spread batter evenly by rolling wrist to tilt tin. Return to grill for 5 minutes or until lightly brown. Repeat until batter is used up.

- After last layer, turn out and leave to cool on a wire rack.

Moist Walnut Apple Cake

Preparation time: 15 minutes   Baking time: 70–80 minutes   Oven setting: 175°C / 350°F

Ingredients

Plain (all-purpose) flour	125 g
Self-raising flour	125 g
Ground cinnamon	1 tsp
Baking powder	1 tsp
Bicarbonate of soda	1 tsp
Salt	¼ tsp
Brown sugar	200 g
Corn oil	125 ml
Canned apple pie filling	595 g
Large eggs	2, beaten
Vanilla essence	1 tsp
Chopped walnuts	½ cup
Raisins	½ cup

Method

- Grease sides and line base of a 23-cm round cake tin with greaseproof paper and grease again. Preheat oven to 170°C / 350°F.

- Sift plain flour and self-raising flour, ground cinnamon powder, baking powder and bicarbonate of soda together into a bowl of an electric mixer fitted with a mixer. Add salt and sugar and mix.

- Add corn oil and apple pie filling, followed by beaten egg and vanilla essence. Beat for 1 minute.

- Pour batter into prepared cake tin. Bake for 70–80 minutes or until a skewer inserted into the centre of cake comes out clean.

Carrot Cake

Preparation time: 20 minutes   Baking time: 45 minutes   Oven setting: 165°C / 325°F

Ingredients

Castor (superfine) sugar	225 g
Corn oil	250 ml
Eggs	3, large
Plain (all-purpose) flour	150 g
Baking powder	$1^{1}/_{2}$ tsp
Bicarbonate of soda	$1^{1}/_{3}$ tsp
Ground cinnamon	$1^{1}/_{3}$ tsp
Salt	$^{1}/_{2}$ tsp
Carrot	250 g, grated
Chopped nuts	125 g

Method

- Line a 22-cm square cake tin with greaseproof paper and grease well. Preheat oven to 165°C / 325°F.

- Beat sugar in corn oil. Beat in eggs one at a time. Sift in dry ingredients. Add salt and fold into mixture. Stir in grated carrot and chopped nuts.

- Pour batter into prepared tin. Bake for about 45 minutes or until skewer inserted into the centre of cake comes out clean.

Peach Custard Sandwich Cake

Preparation time: 15 minutes   Cooking time: 10 minutes   Baking time: 10–15 minutes   Oven setting: 175°C / 350°F

Ingredients

Corn oil	1 Tbsp
Rum	1 Tbsp
Peach syrup	2 Tbsp
Eggs	4, large
Castor (superfine) sugar	115 g
Self-raising flour	120 g, sifted
Canned sliced peaches	1 can (870 g)

Custard Cream

Cornflour (cornstarch)	40 g
Custard powder	40 g
Milk (A)	115 ml
Milk (B)	450 ml
Sugar	115 g
Butter	45 g
Egg	1, well beaten
Vanilla essence	1 tsp
Peach syrup	1 Tbsp
Rum	1 Tbsp

Method

- Line two 18 x 27-cm cake tins with greaseproof paper and grease well. Preheat oven to 175°C / 350°F.

- Combine corn oil, rum and 1 Tbsp syrup. Set aside.

- Whisk eggs and sugar until light and fluffy. Sift in sifted flour. Fold quickly. Stir in corn-oil mixture.

- Divide batter equally between the two prepared cake tins. Bake for 10–15 minutes or until golden. Drizzle remaining syrup over cakes.

- While cakes are baking, prepare custard cream. Blend cornflour, custard powder and milk (A) and set aside. Bring milk (B), sugar and butter to the boil in a saucepan. Add custard mixture, stirring constantly until mixture thickens. Remove from heat. Beat in egg, vanilla essence, peach syrup and rum.

- Sandwich cakes with custard cream and spread remaining cream over top and sides of cake as desired. Arrange peach slices decoratively on cake. If preferred, cake can be served chilled.

Honey Sour Cream Cake

Preparation time: 15 minutes   Baking time: 45–50 minutes   Oven setting: 165°C / 325°F

Ingredients

Plain (all-purpose) flour	300 g
Bicarbonate of soda	2 tsp
Baking powder	$^1/_2$ tsp
Ground cinnamon	1 tsp
Ground nutmeg	1 tsp
Salt	$^1/_4$ tsp
Corn oil	115 ml
Brown sugar	225 g
Large eggs	4, yolks and whites separated
Honey	175 ml
Sour cream	300 g
Chopped nuts	125 g

Method

- Line and grease base of a 25–27-cm tube pan. Preheat oven to 165°C / 325°F.

- Sift flour, bicarbonate of soda, baking powder, ground cinnamon and nutmeg together. Add salt. Set aside.

- Cream corn oil and sugar. Beat in egg yolks one at a time until light and creamy. Beat in honey. Fold in sifted ingredients alternately with sour cream. Stir in nuts.

- Beat egg whites until just stiff. Fold into batter one-third at a time.

- Pour batter into prepared tin. Bake for 45–50 minutes or until a skewer inserted into the centre of cake comes out clean.

Orange Prune Cake

Preparation time: 20 minutes   Baking time: 45–50 minutes   Oven setting: 165°C / 325°F

Ingredients

Butter	250 g, cut into cubes
Castor (superfine) sugar	210 g
Orange rind	grated from 2 oranges
Vanilla essence	1 tsp
Large eggs	4
Self-raising flour	250 g, sifted
Lukewarm water	3 Tbsp
Dried prunes	120 g, pitted and chopped

Method

- Line a 22-cm square cake tin with greaseproof paper and grease well. Preheat oven to 165°C / 325°F.

- Cream butter and sugar until light and fluffy. Add orange rind and vanilla essence. Beat until well combined.

- Add eggs one at a time, beating well after each addition. Fold in flour a little at a time. Stir in water. Add chopped prunes.

- Pour batter into prepared tin. Bake on centre shelf for 45–50 minutes or until a skewer inserted into the centre of cake comes out clean.

- This cake keeps well for 2–3 days in an airtight container.

Crunchy-Top Cake

Preparation time: 15 minutes   Baking time: 40 minutes   Oven setting: 175°C / 350°F

Ingredients

Butter	250 g, cut into cubes
Castor (superfine) sugar	210 g
Orange rind	grated from 1 orange
Lemon rind	grated from 1 lemon
Large eggs	4
Self-raising flour	240 g
Orange juice or milk	1 Tbsp
Demerara (pale brown granulated) sugar	60 g

Method

- Line a 20-cm round cake tin with greaseproof paper and grease well. Preheat oven to 175°C / 350°F.

- Cream butter and sugar until light and fluffy. Add orange and lemon rind. Add eggs one at a time, beating well after each addition. Sift in half the flour, then stir. Repeat with other half. Stir in orange juice or milk.

- Spoon batter into prepared tin. Even out surface. Bake on centre shelf for 25 minutes.

- Without removing cake from oven, sprinkle demerara sugar over the top. Bake for another 15 minutes or until cake is done. A skewer inserted into the centre of cake should come out clean.

Surprise Cake

Preparation time: 20 minutes   Baking time: 50 minutes   Oven setting: 175°C / 350°F

Ingredients

Butter	250 g, cut into cubes
Castor (superfine) sugar	210 g
Vanilla essence	1 tsp
Lemon essence	1 tsp
Large eggs	3
Self-raising flour	240 g, sifted
Salt	1 pinch
Pineapple juice	2 Tbsp

Pineapple Topping

Butter	120 g, cut into cubes
Brown sugar	115 g
Cornflakes	30 g, crushed
Canned pineapple	1 can (565 g), chopped
Desiccated coconut	30 g

Method

- Line a 22-cm round cake tin with greaseproof paper. Preheat oven to 175°C / 350°F.

- Prepare pineapple topping. Cream butter and brown sugar until creamy. Add cornflakes, pineapple and coconut. Set aside.

- Prepare cake batter. Cream butter and sugar until light and creamy. Add essences. Beat in eggs one at a time. Fold in sifted flour. Add salt. Mix in pineapple juice.

- Spoon half the batter into prepared tin. Spoon half the pineapple topping over batter and spread evenly. Repeat with other halves to form four alternating layers. Bake for 40–45 minutes or until cake is golden.

- Remove cake from oven and quickly spoon 2 Tbsp pineapple juice over the top. Switch oven setting to grill, then return cake to oven for 10–12 minutes or until topping turns light brown.

Cranberry Walnut Brownie

Preparation time: 40 minutes   Baking time: 28–30 minutes   Oven setting: 175°C / 350°F

Ingredients

Dried cranberries	80 g, chopped
Unsweetened cranberry juice	6 Tbsp
Plain (all-purpose) flour	200 g
Ground cinnamon	½ tsp
Butter	200 g, at room temperature
Dark chocolate (55%)	300 g
Dark brown sugar	275 g
Vanilla essence	1 tsp
Medium eggs	4, each about 65 g
Walnuts	100 g, chopped

Method

- In a small bowl, soaked chopped cranberries in cranberry juice for at least 30 minutes. Drain and reserve 5 Tbsp juice for use in cake.

- Line a 26.5 x 18-cm baking tin with greaserpoof paper. Sift flour and ground cinnamon together. Preheat oven to 175°C / 350°F.

- In a medium non-stick saucepan, add butter, dark chocolate, brown sugar and reserved juice. Warm over low heat, stirring until butter and chocolate are melted and evenly mixed. Stir in vanilla essence. Remove from heat and allow to cool to lukewarm.

- Using a handheld electric mixer, beat eggs into chocolate mixture one at a time. Beat each egg for 15 seconds.

- Fold in sifted flour and drained cranberries.

- Spread half the batter into prepared baking tin and scatter with chopped walnuts. Cover with remaining batter and level surface.

- Bake for 28–30 minutes or until edges of cake are springy to the touch and centre has a slight "give in". A skewer inserted into the centre of cake will emerge slightly sticky.

- Remove and leave cake to cool in pan for 1 hour before turning out onto a wire rack to cool completely.

- Cut into squares or slabs and serve. If not serving immediately, store in an airtight container in the fridge.

Tea Cake

Preparation time: 25 minutes   Baking time: 50 minutes   Oven setting: 175°C / 350°F

Ingredients

Mixed fruit	250 g, chopped
Mixed peel	120 g, chopped
Cooled strong tea	125 ml
Self-raising flour	240 g
Ground cinnamon	1 tsp
Ground nutmeg	1 tsp
Butter	180 g, cut into cubes
Brown sugar	180 g
Orange rind	grated from 1–2 oranges
Large eggs	2

Method

- Soak mixed fruit and peel in cooled strong tea overnight.

- On baking day, line a 20-cm square cake tin with greaseproof paper and grease well. Preheat oven to 175°C / 350°F.

- Sift flour, cinnamon and nutmeg together. Set aside.

- Beat butter and sugar until light and creamy. Add orange rind. Beat in eggs one at a time. Add tea-soaked ingredients. Fold in sifted ingredients.

- Spread batter evenly in prepared cake tin. Bake for 50 minutes or until a skewer inserted into the centre of cake comes out clean.

Note:

A packet of fruit mix (375 g) can be used in place of the mixed fruit and mixed peel in this recipe.

Melt Away Chocolate Roll

Preparation time: 20 minutes   Baking time: 20–25 minutes   Oven setting: 175°C / 350°F

Ingredients

Large eggs	5, yolks and whites separated
Castor (superfine) sugar	180 g
Cream of tartar	¼ tsp
Vanilla essence	¼ tsp
Salt	¼ tsp
Plain (all-purpose) flour	30 g
Cocoa powder	45 g
Baking powder	½ tsp
Icing sugar	as needed

Whipped Cream

Cold whipping cream	200 ml
Icing sugar	2 Tbsp, sifted
Vanilla essence	1 tsp

Method

- Line a 30-cm square Swiss roll tray with greaseproof paper and grease well. Preheat oven to 175°C / 350°F.

- Whisk egg whites with half the sugar and cream of tartar until just stiff.

- Whisk egg yolks with remaining sugar, vanilla essence and salt until thick and lemon-coloured.

- Sift flour, cocoa and baking powder twice, then lightly fold into egg yolk mixture. Carefully fold in beaten egg whites until just incorporated.

- Pour batter into prepared tray and bake for 20–25 minutes.

- Sift icing sugar onto a clean tea towel and turn baked cake onto it. Peel off greaseproof paper and gently roll cake up with the help of the tea towel. Let cake sit until cooled.

- In the meantime, prepare whipped cream. Place a mixer bowl and whisk in the freezer for at least 20 minutes to chill. Place whipping cream, icing sugar and vanilla essence in the cold bowl and whisk on high speed for about 1 minute until medium peaks form. Be careful not to over beat.

- Gently unroll cake and spread with whipped cream, then carefully roll up again. Trim edges to neaten cake. Sift extra icing sugar over roll, if desired.

- Chill well before serving.

Cinnamon Roll

Preparation time: 15 minutes   Baking time: 12–15 minutes   Oven setting: 190°C / 375°F

Ingredients

Cornflour	60 g
Plain (all-purpose) flour	30 g
Baking powder	2 tsp
Ground cinnamon	2 tsp
Large eggs	3
Castor (superfine) sugar	90 g
Vanilla essence	1 tsp

Honey Spread

Butter	90 g
Honey	3 Tbsp

Method

- Line a 27-cm square Swiss roll tin with greaseproof paper and grease well. Preheat oven to 190°C / 350°F.

- Sift flours, baking powder and cinnamon together. Set aside.

- Whisk eggs until light and fluffy. Gradually beat in sugar. Add vanilla essence. Sift in sifted ingredients. Fold gently.

- Spread batter evenly in prepared tin. Bake for 12–15 minutes until golden brown and springy to the touch.

- Turn baked cake out onto a clean tea towel. Peel off greaseproof paper and gently roll cake up with the help of the tea towel. Let cake sit until cooled.

- In the meantime, prepare honey spread. Beat butter until light and creamy. Add honey, 1 Tbsp at a time. Mix until incorporated.

- Gently unroll cake and spread with honey spread and roll up again. Trim edges to neaten cake.

Coffee Brandy Sponge

Preparation time: 45 minutes   Baking time: 25 minutes   Oven setting: 175°C / 350°F

Ingredients

Cornflour	60 g
Plain (all-purpose) flour	60 g
Baking powder	2 tsp
Coffee	2 tsp
Water	2 tsp
Brandy	1 Tbsp
Large eggs	4
Castor (superfine) sugar	115 g
Corn oil	2 Tbsp

Coffee Cream

Coffee	2 tsp
Brandy	1 Tbsp
Cold butter	250 g, cut into small pieces
Icing sugar	150 g, sifted
Vanilla essence	1 tsp
Evaporated milk	1 small can (170 g), chilled

Method

- Line two 21-cm round cake tins with greaseproof paper and grease well. Preheat oven to 175°C / 350°F.

- Sift flours and baking powder together. Set aside.

- Combine coffee, water and brandy. Set aside.

- Whisk eggs and sugar until light and fluffy. Sift in sifted ingredients a little at a time. Quickly but carefully fold into egg mixture. Add corn oil and coffee mixture.

- Divide batter equally between prepared tins. Bake for 25 minutes or until cakes are springy to the touch. Leave cakes to cool slightly before unmmoulding. Place on a wire rack to cool completely.

- In the meantime, prepare coffee cream. Combine coffee and brandy. Set aside. Cream butter and sugar until light and creamy. Add vanilla essence. Beat in cold milk a little at a time. Add coffee and brandy mixture and mix well.

- Slice cooled cakes horizontally. Sandwich with coffee cream.

- Spread coffee cream on top surface of one cake sandwich. Place other cake sandwich on top to form a tall four layer cake.

- Coat and pipe top and sides with remaining coffee cream. Chill before serving.

Honey-Crusted Banana Cake

Preparation time: 15 minutes   Baking time: 45 minutes   Oven setting: 175°C / 350°F

Ingredients

Butter	250 g, cut into cubes
Castor (superfine) sugar	170 g
Vanilla essence	$^1/_2$ tsp
Large eggs	4
Ripe bananas (*pisang rastali*)	4 medium or 5 small, peeled and finely mashed
Self-raising flour	240 g
Milk	1 Tbsp

Honey Topping

Butter	45 g
Honey	1 Tbsp
Brown sugar	45 g
Ground cinnamon	$^1/_2$ tsp
Rum or brandy (optional)	1 tsp

Method

- Line a 22-cm round cake tin with greaseproof paper and grease well. Preheat oven to 175°C / 350°F.

- Cream butter, sugar and vanilla essence until light and fluffy. Beat in eggs one at a time. Add mashed bananas. Sift in half the flour. Carefully fold into mixture. Repeat with other half. Stir in milk to achieve a soft, dropping consistency.

- Pour batter into prepared tin. Bake for 35 minutes.

- In the meantime, cream butter with honey and sugar until light and fluffy. Add cinnamon, then rum or brandy if desired.

- Remove cake from oven and keep oven on. Quickly spread honey topping on surface of cake, then return to the oven to bake for 10 minutes or until topping is set.

- Let cake cool in tin before unmoulding.

Dreamy Cheesecake

Preparation time: 25 minutes   Baking time: 25 minutes   Oven setting: 175°C / 350°F

Ingredients

Butter	180 g, cut into cubes
Icing sugar	150 g, sifted
Vanilla essence	$1/2$ tsp
Egg yolks	2
Egg white	1
Self-raising flour	150 g, sifted
Cold water	75 ml
Melted chocolate (optional)	

Cheese Topping

Cream cheese	250 g, at room temperature
Egg yolks	2
Castor (superfine) sugar	4 Tbsp
Vanilla essence	1 tsp
Lemon essence	1 tsp
Egg whites	4

Method

- Line the base of a 21–22-cm round springform cake tin with greaseproof paper and grease well. Preheat oven to 175°C / 350°F.

- Cream butter and sugar until light and fluffy. Add vanilla essence. Beat in egg yolks one at a time, followed by egg white. Fold in sifted flour alternately with water until batter is of a dropping consistency. Add a little more water if necessary.

- Pour batter into prepared tin and smoothern surface. Bake for 25–30 minutes.

- In the meantime, prepare cheese topping. Beat cream cheese until smooth. Beat in egg yolks one at a time. Add sugar and essences and beat until sugar is dissolved. Set aside. Whisk egg whites until soft peaks form. Fold lightly into cream cheese mixture.

- Remove cake from oven. Add cheese topping and spread evenly. Grill for about 10 minutes or until topping is firm to the touch. To prevent top surface from browning, cover with a flat tin lid.

- Let cake cool before serving. Coat cake with melted chocolate if desired.

Cotton Cheesecake

Preparation and waiting time: 1 hour 30 minutes   Baking time: 1 hour 20 minutes   Oven setting: 160°C / 320°F

Ingredients

Cake flour	60 g
Cornflour	20 g
Fresh milk	200 ml
Cream cheese	310 g, room temperature
Butter	90 g, room temperature
Lemon juice	1 Tbsp
Vanilla essence	1 tsp
Large egg yolks	5
Large egg whites	5
Cream of tartar	¼ tsp
Castor sugar	140 g
Whipping cream	200 ml
Strawberries or any fresh fruit	for decorating
Icing sugar	for dusting

Method

- Prepare a 23-cm round cake tin and a 27–28 cm round pan to hold the cake tin.

- Line cake tin with greaseproof paper and grease well. Sift cake flour and cornflour together. Set aside.

- Place milk and cream cheese in a large heatproof bowl over simmering water. Stir constantly until melted and thickened. Remove from heat. Using a handheld electric mixer, lightly whisk until evenly blended and smooth.

- Beat in butter, lemon juice and vanilla essence. Set aside to cool before beating in sifted flours.

- Preheat oven to 160°C / 320°F. Place prepared round pan on the centre shelf of the oven. Fill with water until it comes 2.5 cm up the sides of pan.

- Place egg yolks in a small jug and whisk lightly with the handheld electric mixer. Gradually beat whisked egg yolks into cream cheese mixture.

- Place egg whites and cream of tartar in a mixing bowl and whisk using the handheld electric mixer until frothy. Gradually add sugar, one-third at a time, and whisk until stiff peaks form.

- Fold a quarter of egg white mixture into cream cheese mixture, then fold in remaining mixture one third at a time until well-combined.

- Pour mixture into lined cake tin and place in pan of hot water. Bake for 1 hour 20 minutes or until top of cake is golden brown and firm.

- Leave oven door slightly ajar and let cake sit in oven for 1 hour. Remove from oven and leave cake to cool for 10–15 minutes before turning out onto a wire rack to cool completely.

- Meanwhile, whip cream in a chilled bowl with the hand-mixer until thickened and firm enough for piping.

- Decorate cake with whipped cream and strawberries or any fruit of choice. Dust with icing sugar and serve chilled.

Layer Delight

Preparation time: 40 minutes   Cooking time: 5 minutes   Baking time: 15 minutes   Oven setting: 190°C / 375°F

Ingredients

Large eggs	4
Castor (superfine) sugar	90 g
Vanilla essence	1 tsp
Self-raising flour	120 g, sifted
Corn oil	1 Tbsp
Milk	1 Tbsp
Rum	1–2 Tbsp

Rum Cream

Seedless raisins	180 g
Rum	4 Tbsp
Cold butter	250 g, cut into small cubes
Icing sugar	150 g, sifted
Vanilla essence	1 tsp
Evaporated milk	1 small can (170 g), chilled

Method

- Grease and flour two 20-cm round cake tins. Preheat oven to 190°C / 375°F.

- Whisk eggs, sugar and vanilla essence until light and fluffy. Sift in sifted flour and fold quickly. Stir in corn oil and milk.

- Divide mixture equally between prepared tins. Bake for 15 minutes.

- Remove cakes from oven. Carefully spoon rum over cakes while still hot. Leave to cool slightly on a wire rack before removing from tins and leaving to cool completely.

- In the meantime, prepare rum cream. Place raisins and 3 Tbsp rum in a small saucepan. Bring to the boil over low heat, then leave to cool. Cream butter and sugar until light and creamy. Add vanilla essence. Beat in evaporated milk a little at a time until incorporated. Beat in remaining rum. Spoon half the cream into another bowl and add raisins. Mix well.

- Sandwich cakes with rum cream (with raisins), then coat cake with remaining cream (without raisins).

Coffee Cake

Preparation time: 15 minutes   Baking time: 35–40 minutes   Oven setting: 175°C / 350°F

Ingredients

Self-raising flour	120 g
Plain (all-purpose) flour	60 g
Bicarbonate of soda	1 tsp
Instant coffee granules	3 tsp
Milk	1 Tbsp
Corn oil	250 ml
Sugar	170 g
Large eggs	3

Coffee Topping

Butter	45 g
Brown sugar	2 Tbsp
Coffee	1 Tbsp

Method

- Line a 22-cm square cake tin with greaseproof paper and grease well. Preheat oven to 175°C / 350°F.

- Sift flours and bicarbonate of soda together. Set aside.

- Dissolve instant coffee granules in milk. Set aside.

- Beat corn oil and sugar together. Add eggs one at a time and beat until well mixed. Fold in sifted flour mixture. Stir in coffee mixture.

- Pour batter into prepared tin. Bake for 25 minutes.

- In the meantime, prepare coffee topping. Cream butter and sugar until light and creamy. Stir in coffee.

- Remove cake from oven and leave oven on. Quickly spread coffee topping on top and return cake to oven. Bake for 10–15 minutes or until topping bubbles and turns dark brown.

- Let cake cool in tin before unmoulding.

Family Favourite Custard Flan

Preparation time: 20 minutes   Cooking time: 15 minutes   Baking time: 15 minutes   Oven Setting: 190°C / 375°F

Ingredients

Plain (all-purpose) flour	45 g
Cornflour	15 g
Baking powder	3/4 tsp
Eggs	2, large
Castor (superfine) sugar	55 g
Vanilla essence	1/2 tsp
Corn oil	1/2 Tbsp
Coconut cream	1 Tbsp
Chocolate rice	as needed

Custard Topping

Custard powder	30 g
Coconut cream	225 ml, extracted from 1/2 grated coconut and sufficient water
Coconut milk	340 ml, extracted from same 1/2 grated coconut and sufficient water
Sugar	75 g
Salt	a pinch
Vanilla essence	1/2 tsp

Method

- Grease and flour a 21-cm round spring cake tin. Preheat oven to 190°C / 375°F.

- Sift flours and baking powder together.

- Whisk eggs, sugar and vanilla essence until light and fluffy. Sift in sifted ingredients and fold in quickly. Stir in corn oil and coconut cream.

- Pour batter into prepared tin and even out surface. Bake for 15 minutes or until well risen and top is lightly browned. Leave to cool in tin.

- In the meantime, prepare custard topping. Stir custard powder into a little coconut milk until dissolved. Pour into a saucepan and add remaining coconut milk, sugar and salt. Stir over low heat. When mixture is near boiling, add coconut cream and vanilla essence. Continue stirring until mixture starts to bubble and boil. Remove from heat.

- Pour custard topping over cooled cake and set aside to cool. Ssprinkle with chocolate rice. Serve chilled.

Note:

Coconut cream, or thick coconut milk, is the liquid produced by pressing or squeezing grated coconut for the first time, sometimes with water added. Coconut milk, or thin coconut milk, is the liquid produced by second and subsequent pressings, often with water added.

Papaya Sponge Flan

Preparation time: 15 minutes   Cooking time: 30 minutes   Baking time: 10–15 minutes   Oven setting: 190°C / 375°F

Ingredients

Cornflour	45 g
Plain (all-purpose) flour	15 g
Baking powder	$^3/_4$ tsp
Eggs	2
Castor (superfine) sugar	55 g
Lemon essence	$^1/_2$ tsp
Corn oil	1 Tbsp
Milk	2 tsp

Papaya Topping

Gelatine	2 Tbsp
Hot water	115 ml
Ripe papaya	1, about 1 kg, skinned and seeded, cut into cubes
Orange rind	grated from 1 orange
Sugar	115 g
Lemon essence	1 tsp
Vanilla essence	1 tsp
Cream	1 small can (170 g)

Method

- Grease a 21-cm round springform cake tin. Preheat oven to 190°C / 375°F.

- Sift flours and baking powder together. Set aside.

- Whisk eggs, sugar and lemon essence until light and fluffy. Sift in sifted ingredients. Fold through quickly and evenly. Stir in corn oil and milk.

- Pour batter into prepared tin. Bake for 10–15 minutes or until cake springs back when lightly touched with a finger. Leave cake to cool in tin.

- In the meantime, prepare papaya topping. Sprinkle gelatine over the hot water and set aside to bloom. Place papaya and orange rind in a blender and process. Pour into a saucepan, then cover and cook over medium heat, stirring occasionally. When papaya pulp is reduced to about $2^1/_2$–3 cups, remove from heat. Stir in sugar and essences. Stir in bloomed gelatine. Whisk cream until firm peaks form. Fold lightly into papaya mixture.

- Pour papaya topping over cooled cake. Refrigerate until firm before removing from tin.

Agar-Agar Flan Delight

Preparation time: 15 minutes   Cooking time: 15 minutes   Baking time: 15 minutes   Oven setting: 190°C / 375°F

Ingredients

Large eggs	2
Castor (superfine) sugar	55 g
Vanilla essence	$^1/_2$ tsp
Self-raising flour	60 g
Corn oil	$^1/_2$ Tbsp
Milk	$^1/_2$ Tbsp
Glacé cherries	2–3

Agar-agar topping

Agar-agar strips	7 g
Water	340 ml
Sugar	115 g
Vanilla essence	1 tsp
Red food colouring	2–3 drops
Egg white	1, large

Method

- Grease a 20–22-cm flan tin. Preheat oven to 190°C / 375°F.

- Whisk eggs, sugar and vanilla essence until thick and pale. Sift in flour and fold in quickly. Stir in corn oil and milk.

- Pour mixture into prepared flan tin. Bake for 15 minutes or until golden. Let cake cool before turning out.

- In the meantime, prepare agar-agar topping. Rinse agar-agar strips, then boil in water. Add sugar and stir until dissolved. Remove from heat. Stir in vanilla essence and food colouring. Leave to cool. Beat egg white until just stiff. Strain jelly mixture into egg white, while whisking at the same time.

- Pour agar-agar topping onto cooled cake. When topping cools, decorate with cherries. Chill before serving.

COOKIES

Sesame Cookies

Preparation time: 40 minutes   Baking time: 15 minutes   Oven setting: 175°C / 350°F   Makes 50

Ingredients

Plain (all-purpose) flour	120 g
Self-raising flour	120 g
Vegetable shortening	180 g
Castor (superfine) sugar	170 g
Egg yolk	1
Salt	$^1/_4$ tsp
Lemon essence	1 tsp
Milk	1 Tbsp
Sesame seeds	175 g, washed and oven-toasted

Method

- Grease or line baking trays. Preheat oven to 175°C / 350°F.

- Sift flours together. Set aside.

- Cream vegetable shortening and sugar. Beat in egg yolk until creamy.
  Add salt and lemon essence. Gradually fold in sifted ingredients. Stir in milk.

- Shape teaspoonfuls of mixture into balls. Roll balls in sesame seeds.
  Place on prepared trays.

- Bake for 15–20 minutes or until lightly browned.

- Leave to cool slightly on trays before placing on wire racks to cool completely.
  Store in airtight containers.

Better Than Best Chocolate Chip Cookies

Preparation time: 30 minutes   Baking time: 18–20 minutes   Oven setting: 160°C / 320°F   Makes 25

Ingredients

Plain (all-purpose) flour	180 g
Cornflour	10 g
Baking powder	½ tsp
Bicarbonate of soda	½ tsp
Butter	125 g, at room temperature
Sugar	80 g
Light brown sugar	80 g
Medium egg	1, about 65 g
Vanilla essence	1 tsp
Salt	½ tsp
Chocolate chips	200 g
Walnuts	100 g, toasted and coarsely chopped

Method

- Grease or line baking trays. Preheat oven to 160°C / 320°F.

- Sift flour, cornflour, baking powder and bicarbonate of soda together.

- Cream butter and sugars until creamy. Add egg, vanilla essence and salt. Beat well.

- Stir in sifted flour mixture, followed by chocolate chips and chopped walnuts.

- Use a small ice cream scoop to scoop mixture into 25 rounds. Roll into balls and flatten slightly. Place on baking trays, keeping them 5 cm apart. Refrigerate for 30 minutes.

- Bake for 18–20 minutes, or until light golden brown.

- Leave to cool on trays for 10 minutes before placing on wire racks to cool completely. Store in airtight containers.

Chocolate Crinkles

Preparation time: 30 minutes   Baking time: 15 minutes   Oven setting: 175°C / 350°F   Makes 50

Ingredients

Plain (all-purpose) flour	240 g
Baking powder	1 tsp
Unsweetened cocoa powder	30 g
Butter	180 g, cut into cubes
Icing sugar	180 g
Egg yolks	2
Raisins	120 g, chopped
Chopped nuts of choice	60 g
Salt	a pinch

Method

- Grease or line baking trays. Preheat oven to 175°C / 350°F.

- Sift flour, baking powder and cocoa powder together. Set aside.

- Cream butter and sugar until creamy. Beat in egg yolks. Stir in raisins and nuts. Gradually fold in sifted ingredients and salt.

- Shape into small balls. You should get about 50 pieces. Place on baking trays.

- Bake for 15 minutes.

- Leave to cool on trays for 10 minutes before placing on wire racks to cool completely. Store in airtight containers.

Pistachio Shortbread

Preparation time: 20 minutes   Baking time: 15–18 minutes   Oven setting: 140°C / 285°F   Makes 125

Ingredients

Plain (all-purpose) flour	520 g
Baking powder	2 tsp
Bicarbonate of soda	½ tsp
Cornflour	60 g
Butter	360 g, at room temperature
Vanilla essence	2 tsp
Icing sugar	160 g, sifted
Milk	2 Tbsp
Pistachios	2½ Tbsp, coarsely chopped

Method

- Prepare dough a day ahead as it requires chilling overnight.

- Sift flour, baking powder, bicarbonate of soda and cornflour together and set aside.

- Cream butter, vanilla and icing sugar together until light and fluffy. Beat in milk, then add sifted ingredients and beat on low speed until just combined.

- Divide dough into 2 equal portions. Place on a plastic sheet and roll each portion out into a 30-cm log. Cover with cling wrap and refrigerate overnight.

- When ready to bake, grease or line baking trays. Preheat oven to 140°C / 285°F.

- Cut dough into 0.5-cm thick slices and arrange on baking trays. You should get about 125 pieces.

- Sprinkle with chopped pistachios and lightly press nuts into dough.

- Bake for 15–18 minutes or until lightly golden.

- Leave to cool on trays for 10 minutes before placing on wire racks to cool completely. Store in airtight containers.

Note:

If using a multi-tier oven, bake the first tray for 5 minutes, then turn it around and place on lower shelf before putting another tray on top to bake for the full 15–18 minutes.

Cornflake Crunchies

Preparation time: 30 minutes   Baking time: 12 minutes   Oven setting: 175°C / 350°F   Makes 34

Ingredients

Butter	105 g
Sugar	115 g
Egg yolk	1
Self-raising flour	90 g
Plain (all-purpose) flour	30 g
Raisins	100 g
Cornflakes	

Method

- Grease or line baking trays. Preheat oven to 175°C / 350°F.

- Cream butter and sugar until light and fluffy. Beat in egg yolk. Sift in flours. Mix well. Stir in raisins.

- Roll teaspoonfuls of mixture in lightly crushed cornflakes. You should get about 34 pieces.Place on prepared trays.

- Bake for 12–15 minutes until lightly browned.

- Leave to cool on trays for 10 minutes before placing on wire racks to cool completely. Store in airtight containers.

Nut Fingers

Preparation time: 60 minutes   Baking time: 20 minutes   Oven setting: 175°C / 350°F   Makes 24 pairs

Ingredients

Plain (all-purpose) flour	210 g
Baking powder	2 tsp
Castor (superfine) sugar	90 g
Vanilla essence	$^3/_4$ tsp
Salt	1 pinch
Egg yolk	1
Egg white	1, halved
Cold butter	105 g, cut into small cubes
Peanuts	as needed
Jam of choice	as needed

Method

- Grease or line baking trays. Preheat oven to 175°C / 350°F.

- Sift flour and baking powder into a mixing bowl. Add sugar, vanilla essence, salt, egg yolk and $^1/_2$ egg white. Stir to mix well.

- Add butter and blend with a pastry cutter or knife. Work with fingers to form a soft dough.

- On a floured work surface, roll dough into a 3-mm thick rectangle. Cut 10 x 1-cm fingers.

- Carefully transfer fingers onto baking trays, lifting with a flat, broad-bladed knife. Brush with remaining egg white. Decorate with peanuts.

- Bake for 20 minutes or until golden brown. Remove and leave to cool.

- Sandwich jam between two fingers. Store in airtight containers.

Cheese Ropes

Preparation time: 45 minutes   Baking time: 12 minutes   Oven setting: 175°C / 350°F   Makes 40

Ingredients

Butter	60 g
Cream cheese	60 g, at room temperature
Egg	1
Salt	$^1/_2$ tsp
Ground white pepper	a dash
Plain (all-purpose) flour	180 g
Baking powder	1 tsp

Method

• Prepare 2–3 baking trays. Preheat oven to 175°C / 350°F.

• Beat butter and cheese until creamy. Beat in egg. Add salt and pepper. Sift in flour and baking powder. Mix to form soft dough.

• On a lightly floured work surface, roll out dough. Cut into 1-cm wide strips. Shape each strip into a long and thin roll, then cut into 12–13-cm lengths You should get about 80 pieces.

• Hold two lengths together, one hand at each end. Twist by turning ends in opposite directions. Place on ungreased trays. At each end, lightly press against tray to prevent unwinding.

• Bake for 12–15 minutes or until golden. Transfer to a wire rack to cool. Store in airtight containers.

Muruku

Preparation time: 20 minutes   Cooking time: 45 minutes

Ingredients

Rice flour	480 g, sifted
Cumin	1 tsp
Ajowan	1 tsp
Salt	$1^1/_2$ tsp
Baking powder	1 tsp
Butter	30 g, softened at room temperature
Coconut milk	675–900 ml, squeezed from 1 grated coconut and sufficient water

Cooking oil for deep-frying

Method

- Roast rice flour in a wok over low heat for 5 minutes, stirring constantly. Take care not to brown flour. Remove from heat and leave to cool completely, preferably overnight.

- Add cumin, ajowan, salt and baking powder to flour. Add butter last. Gradually pour in enough coconut milk to form stiff dough.

- Heat oil in a wok. Put dough in a cookie press fitted with either a one or a three-star nozzle. Pipe 7–8-cm lengths into hot oil.

- Fry over medium heat until golden brown. Drain on absorbent paper. When cool, store in airtight containers.

Orange Biscuits

Preparation time: 30 minutes   Baking time: 8 minutes   Oven setting: 175°C / 350°F
Makes 80

Ingredients

Self-raising flour	120 g
Plain (all-purpose) flour	30 g
Rice flour	30 g
Butter	120 g
Castor (superfine) sugar	120 g
Orange rind	grated from 1 orange
Salt	a pinch
Egg yolk	1
Orange juice	1 Tbsp

Method

- Grease 2–3 baking trays. Preheat oven to 175°C / 350°F.

- Sift flours together. Set aside.

- Cream butter and sugar until creamy. Add orange rind and salt.

- Sift in sifted flours and fold into creamed mixture. Bind with egg yolk and orange juice.

- Put mixture into a cookie press. Pipe onto greased trays. You should get about 80 cookies.

- Bake for 5–8 minutes or until light golden.

- Leave to cool on trays for 10 minutes before placing on wire racks to cool completely. Store in airtight containers.

SPECIALLY FOR CHILDREN

Bo Peep's Cookie Staffs

Preparation time: 45 minutes   Baking time: 12 minutes   Oven setting: 190°C / 375°F   Makes 30

Ingredients

Butter	120 g, cut into cubes
Brown sugar	120 g
Vanilla essence	$1/2$ tsp
Salt	1 pinch
Egg	1
Plain (all-purpose) flour	240 g
Baking powder	1 tsp
Milk	4 tsp, cold
Egg white	$1/2$, beaten
Hundreds and thousands	

Method

- Grease 2–3 baking trays. Preheat oven to 190°C / 375°F.

- Beat butter and sugar until creamy. Add vanilla essence and salt. Beat in egg. Sift in flour and baking powder. Mix with milk to form soft dough.

- On a lightly floured work surface, roll tablespoonfuls of mixture into pencil-like sticks. Cut into 12–15-cm lengths. You should get about 30. Bend one end of each length to resemble the crook of a cane.

- Place on greased baking trays. Bush with egg white. Sprinkle hundreds and thousands over the top.

- Bake for 12–15 minutes until lightly browned. Carefully transfer to a wire rack to cool. Store in airtight containers.

Coconut Candy

Preparation time: 15 minutes   Cooking time: 30 minutes   Makes 30

Ingredients

Grated skinned coconut	300 g
Sugar	565 g
Evaporated milk	1 small can (170 g)
Butter	45 g
Vanilla essence	1 tsp
Green food colouring	a few drops

Method

- Prepare an 18 x 15-cm tray and grease well.

- Place coconut, sugar and milk in a heavy saucepan. Stir continuously over medium heat until sugar dissolves.

- Stir in butter, vanilla essence and food colouring. Keep stirring until mixture thickens. To test if mixture is ready, drop bits of thickened mixture into a cup of cold water. They should form soft balls.

- Press thickened mixture into prepared tray. Cover with a plastic sheet and use a rolling pin to even out surface. Leave to set and cool.

- When slightly cool, cut into squares. When completely cooled to room temperature, store in airtight containers.

Waffles

Preparation time: 30–45 minutes   Cooking time: 5 minutes per waffle   Makes 8–10

Ingredients

Plain (all-purpose) flour	210 g
Baking powder	1 Tbsp
Castor (superfine) sugar	1 Tbsp
Salt	¾ tsp
Eggs	2, yolks and whites separated
Milk	375 ml
Corn oil	90 ml

Method

- Sift flour and baking powder into a bowl. Stir in sugar and salt. Set aside.

- Using an electric mixer, whisk egg whites until stiff but not dry. Set aside.

- In another bowl, beat egg yolks until thick and lemon-coloured. Continue beating while adding milk and corn oil.

- Add flour mixture and beat until smooth. Fold in beaten egg whites.

- Cover batter with a dry tea towel and set aside for 15–30 minutes.

- Preheat waffle iron on medium-low heat. Add batter and cook according to the manufacturer's instructions.

- Serve waffles hot, topped with your favourite toppings.

Watermelon Agar-Agar

Preparation time: 1 hour   Cooking time: 15 minutes

Ingredients

Agar-agar strips	1½ packets (50 g)
Water	900 ml
Sugar	340 g
Grated coconut	450 g
Pandan leaves	3–4, rinsed and knotted
Egg whites	7 large or 8 medium
Red food colouring	a few drops
Black grass jelly (*chin chow*)	60 g, diced
Green food colouring	a few drops

Method

- Rinse agar-agar strips and place in a saucepan with water and sugar. Bring to the boil.

- While waiting for sugar to dissolve, squeeze grated coconut without adding water to obtain coconut cream. Strain.

- When sugar has dissolved, add pandan leaves and coconut cream. Bring to the boil and remove from heat. Strain into a measuring jug. You should get about 900 ml liquid.

- Whisk egg whites until just stiff. Whisk agar-agar liquid into egg whites until well combined. Pour into a 3-litre, 21-cm bowl or two 18-cm soup bowls.

- When top of jelly is set, use a small knife to cut a circle on the surface, about 2.5 cm from the edge. Add red food colouring to the centre. Carefully mix with fingers, breaking lumps to get an even pink colour. Stir in black jelly to represent melon seeds. Refrigerate until set.

- Remove set agar-agar from the refrigerator and invert onto a dish. Rub green food colouring onto curved surface to represent melon skin.

- Keep refrigerated until ready to serve.

Meringue Drops

Preparation time: 15 minutes   Baking time: 1 hour 30 minutes   Oven setting: 110°C / 225°F   Makes 24

Ingredients

Icing sugar	60 g
Castor (superfine) sugar	60 g
Eggs whites	2
Vanilla essence	$^1/_2$ tsp
Rainbow sprinkles	as desired

Glacé Icing

Icing sugar	120 g, sifted
Water	1 Tbsp, hot
Vanilla essence	2 drops

Method

- Line a cookie tray with greased greaseproof paper. Preheat oven to 110°C / 225°F.

- Combine icing and castor sugars. Set aside.

- Whisk egg whites and vanilla essence until stiff. Gradually beat in half the sugar mixture. Repeat with other half.

- Drop teaspoonfuls of meringue onto prepared tray. You should get about 24 pieces. Bake for 1 hour 30 minutes until firm. Leave to cool before decorating.

- In the meantime, prepare glacé icing. Sift icing sugar into a bowl. Add water and vanilla essence and mix well.

- Dip surface of meringue drops into glacé icing and top with sprinkles as desired.

Note:
To make chocolate meringue, add 1 tsp sifted cocoa powder to the sugar mixture.

Kuih Serimuka

Preparation time: 30 minutes   Cooking time: 45 minutes   Makes 24

Ingredients

Grated coconut	250 g
Water	340 ml
Glutinous rice	450 g
Salt	$1^1/_4$ tsp

Topping

Grated coconut	400 g
Water	225 ml
Pandan juice	55 ml, from pounding and squeezing pandan leaves
Green food colouring	a few drops
Vanilla essence	$^1/_2$ tsp
Eggs	4
Sugar	180 g
Plain (all-purpose) flour	90 g
Tapioca flour	30 g

Method

- Combine grated coconut and water. Squeeze to obtain coconut milk. Strain.

- Rinse glutinous rice and place in a 25–27-cm round pan. Add enough coconut milk to cover rice. Stir in salt. Steam for 20–25 minutes until rice is cooked and tender.

- In the meantime, prepare topping. Mix grated coconut with water and squeeze to obtain about 340 ml coconut milk. Strain and add pandan juice, food colouring and vanilla essence Mix well and set aside.

- Stir eggs and sugar together in a bowl. Do not beat. Sift in flours and mix well. Gradually add coconut milk mixture and stir gently to mix. Strain to remove any lumps.

- When rice is ready, press it firmly down using the back of an oiled spoon. Pour topping over rice. Steam for 20 minutes over medium heat until topping is set.

- Leave to cool before cutting to serve.

PASTRIES

Raisin Pinwheels

Preparation time: 1 hour   Baking time: 15 minutes   Oven setting: 205°C / 400°F   Makes 16

Ingredients

Sugar	3 tsp
Milk	5 Tbsp, warm
Easy blend yeast	10 g
Plain (all-purpose) flour	240 g, sifted
Salt	1 pinch
Butter	30 g, softened, or 2 Tbsp corn oil
Egg	1, beaten
Raisins	60–90 g

Rum Filling

Butter	60 g
Icing sugar	90 g, sifted
Rum	1 Tbsp

Method

- Grease 2–3 baking trays.

- Dissolve sugar in milk. Stir in yeast. Let stand for 15 minutes until frothy.

- Sift flour into a bowl. Add salt. Mix in butter or corn oil. Add yeast liquid and egg. Mix with a wooden spoon. Cover with a damp cloth and let stand for 1 hour or until dough doubles in volume.

- In the meantime, prepare rum filling. Cream butter and icing sugar. Add rum and mix well.

- On a floured work surface, roll dough into a 25 x 20-cm rectangle. Fold evenly into three layers. Repeat process of rolling and folding. Halve dough.

- Roll each half into a 35 x 25-cm rectangle. Spread with rum filling and sprinkle with raisins. Roll up Swiss-roll style. Cut into 2-cm wide slices using a flat-bladed knife.

- Place slices on prepared baking trays. Leave for 15 minutes to rise.

- Preheat oven to 205°C / 400°F and bake for 12–15 minutes until golden. Transfer to a wire rack to cool.

Note:
  As a variation to this recipe, substitute rum with 1 tsp vanilla or lemon essence.

Apple Shortcake

Preparation time: 20 minutes   Baking time: 45–50 minutes   Oven setting: 160°C / 320°F   Makes 12

Ingredients

Plain (all-purpose) flour	350 g
Baking powder	½ tsp
Cold butter	225 g, cut into cubes
Castor (superfine) sugar	100 g
Ground cinnamon	½ tsp, mixed with 1 Tbsp castor (superfine) sugar
Cooking apples	2, peeled, cored and thinly sliced
White sesame seeds	1 tsp

Method

- Line the base of a 23 cm loose-bottom flan tin with greaseproof paper. Preheat oven to 160°C / 320°F.

- Sift flour with baking powder. Set aside.

- Cream butter and sugar until light and fluffy. Stir in flour mixture to get a firm dough.

- Take a little less than half the dough (about 300 g) and roll it into a ball. Place it between two plastic sheets and roll into a circle to fit the base of flan tin. Place dough in the tin.

- Arrange apple slices over dough and sprinkle with cinnamon sugar.

- With your hands, press or roll out remaining dough between two plastic sheets to cover apples.

- Smoothen top using the back of a spoon. Sprinkle with sesame seeds, if desired.

- Bake for 45–50 minutes until lightly golden.

- Leave to cool in tin before cutting into 12 wedges. Serve with clotted cream or ice cream.

Marmalade Hazelnut Slice

Preparation time: 40 minutes   Baking time: 25–30 minutes   Oven setting: 180°C / 360°F   Makes 16

Ingredients

Pastry

Self-raising flour	240 g, sifted
Cold butter	150 g, cut into small cubes
Castor (superfine) sugar	50 g
Egg yolk	1, beaten
Marmalade	6 Tbsp
Hazelnut halves	60 g

Filling

Butter	100 g
Castor (superfine) sugar	100 g
Medium eggs	2
Ground hazelnuts	100 g
Plain (all-purpose) flour	20 g, sifted

Method

- Grease sides and line base of a 30 x 23-cm baking tray.

- Prepare pastry. Place flour into a food processor with butter. Blend until mixture turns crumbly. Pour mixture into a bowl and stir in sugar.

- Make a well in the centre of mixture and add beaten egg yolk. Mix and form into a ball.

- Press dough onto prepared baking tray and rolling lightly with a small pastry roller. Cover with a cling wrap and chill for 30 minutes.

- Preheat oven to 180°C / 360°F.

- Prepare filling. Cream butter and castor sugar until light and fluffy. Beat in eggs and fold in ground hazelnuts and flour.

- Spread marmalade evenly over chilled dough. Spoon filling over and spread evenly using the back of a spoon. Don't worry too much about the gaps as the mixture will spread when baking. Sprinkle with hazelnut halves.

- Bake for 25–30 minutes or until top is golden.

- Leave to cool slightly before cutting into 16 rectangles. Set aside to cool completely on a wire rack. Store in airtight containers.

Coconut Tarts

Preparation time: 30 minutes   Baking time: 30 minutes   Oven setting: 175°C / 350°F   Makes 30

Ingredients

Cold butter	250 g, cut into small cubes
Castor (superfine) sugar	60 g
Egg yolk	1
Salt	a pinch
Vanilla essence	1 tsp
Plain (all-purpose) flour	270 g, sifted

Coconut Filling

Egg	1
Castor (superfine) sugar	90 g
Desiccated coconut	90 g

Method

- Grease 1–2 shallow muffin tins. Preheat oven to 175°C / 350°F.

- Prepare coconut filling. Whisk egg and sugar until sugar is dissolved. Stir in desiccated coconut and mix well. Set aside.

- Prepare pastry. Beat butter and sugar until creamy. Beat in egg yolk. Add salt and vanilla essence. Fold in sifted flour. Put mixture into a piping bag fitted with a star nozzle.

- Starting from the centre of a cavity, pipe dough in a concentric circle to form base of tart. Repeat to pipe about 30 tart bases.

- Top each tart base with coconut filling.

- Bake for 25–30 minutes until golden brown. Transfer to a wire rack to cool. Turn tarts out and store in airtight containers.

Note:
As a variation to this recipe, replace coconut filling with store-bought pineapple jam for quick and easy pineapple tarts.

Almond Tartlets

Preparation time: 30 minutes   Baking time: 25 minutes   Oven setting: 175°C / 350°F   Makes 4

Ingredients

Pastry

Plain (all-purpose) flour	240 g
Salt	$^1/_2$ tsp
Cold butter	150 g, cut into small cubes
Castor (superfine) sugar	2 tsp
Egg yolks	2, separated
Cold water	1 Tbsp
Evaporated milk	2 tsp

Almond Filling

Butter	90 g
Castor (superfine) sugar	90 g
Almond essence	$^1/_4$ tsp
Small eggs	2
Self-raising flour	90 g, sifted

Method

- Grease four 9–10-cm tartlet tins. Preheat oven to 175°C / 350°F.

- Prepare almond filling. Cream butter, sugar and almond essence until light and fluffy. Beat in eggs one at a time. Fold in flour. Set aside until needed.

- Prepare pastry. Sift flour into a bowl. Add salt. Either rub in butter with fingers or blend with a pastry cutter until mixture resembles fine breadcrumbs. Stir in sugar.

- Lightly beat 1 egg yolk with cold water. Add to dough mixture and knead to get a soft but not sticky dough. Add a little more cold water if needed.

- On a lightly floured work surface, roll out dough and cut into rounds to line tartlet tins. Trim off any excess dough. Fill cavity with almond filling.

- Cut remaining pastry into 0.5-cm wide strips. Lay strips over filling to form a lattice.

- Bake for 25–30 minutes or until light golden.

- Make glaze by beating remaining egg yolk with milk.

- Remove tarts from oven and brush immediately with glaze. Place on a wire rack to cool. These tarts will keep for 3–4 days in airtight containers.

Cherry Clafoutis

Preparation time: 30 minutes   Baking time: 25 minutes   Oven setting: 200°C / 400°F   Makes 12

Ingredients

Pastry

Plain (all-purpose) flour	225 g
Icing sugar	20 g
Cold butter	125 g, diced
Egg yolks	2, beaten with 2 Tbsp cold water

Filling

Large eggs	2
Castor (superfine) sugar	55 g
Vanilla essence	1 tsp
Whipping cream	4 Tbsp
Ground almonds	3 Tbsp
Cointreau or any orange liqueur	1 Tbsp
Melted butter	2 Tbsp
Ripe cherries	225 g, pitted and halved

Icing sugar for dusting

Method

- Prepare pastry. Sift flour and icing sugar into bowl of a food processor. Add butter and process until mixture is crumbly.

- Add egg yolk mixture and mix to form a soft dough. Cover with cling wrap and chill for 30 minutes.

- Grease 12 round tartlet tins, each 9 cm in diameter. Roll out pastry between two plastic sheets and cut out 12 rounds using a 9 cm fluted pastry cutter. Line prepared tins with pastry and chill while preparing filling.

- Preheat oven to 200°C / 400°F.

- Prepare filling. In the bowl of an electric mixer, whisk eggs, sugar, vanilla essence and cream for 1 minute until well combined. Stir in ground almonds, Cointreau and melted butter. Mix well and set aside.

- Arrange cherry halves in pastry cases and spoon over filling. Bake for 15–20 minutes or until filling is set.

- Serve warm. Dust with icing sugar and top with whipped cream, if desired.

Sardine Rolls

Preparation time: 30 minutes   Cooking time: 10 minutes   Baking time: 20–25 minutes   Oven setting: 190°C / 375°F   Makes 25

Ingredients

Pastry

Pastry margarine	180 g, at room temperature
Kalamansi lime juice	from 2 limes
Cold water	175 ml, cold
Salt	1/4 tsp
Plain (all-purpose) flour	480 g
Baking powder	1 1/2 tsp
Cold butter	90 g, cut into cubes
Egg	1, beaten
Egg yolk	1, beaten
Cooking oil	3–4 drops

Sardine Filling

Cooking oil	1 Tbsp
Onion	1, peeled and finely chopped
Canned sardines in tomato sauce	150 g, mashed
Red chillies	2, seeded and finely sliced
Green chillies	2, seeded and finely sliced
Ground white pepper	a dash
Kalamansi lime juice	from 4 limes

Method

- Place pastry margarine between two large plastic sheets and roll into a 20 x 15-cm rectangle. Refrigerate.

- Preheat oven to 190°C / 375°F.

- Prepare filling. Heat oil in a wok and fry onion until fragrant. Add remaining ingredients and fry until quite dry. Set aside to cool.

- Combine lime juice, water and salt. Set aside.

- Sift flour and baking powder into a mixing bowl. Add cold butter and blend with a pastry cutter or knife until mixture resembles breadcrumbs. Bind with egg and lime-juice mixture using a wooden spoon.

- Turn mixture out onto a lightly floured work surface and knead to achieve a soft dough. Roll dough into a 40 x 15-cm rectangle.

- Peel plastic sheets from margarine and place in centre of dough rectangle. Fold over ends of dough to cover margarine. Seal edges.

- Roll dough parcel into a rectangle twice as long as it is wide. Fold rectangle into thirds widthwise. Repeat process of rolling and folding twice. Halve dough. Reserve one portion for future use.

- On a lightly floured work surface, roll other half to 2.5-mm thickness. Cut into 10 x 6-cm pieces. Put 1 tsp sardine filling on one short end and roll dough toward the other end. Seal edge with water. Place on ungreased baking trays.

- Bake for 20–25 minutes or until golden brown.

- Make glaze by beating egg yolk and oil together.

- Remove rolls from oven and brush immediately with glaze.

Note:
Store unused dough in a sealed plastic bag and refrigerate or freeze. Frozen pastry will keep for up to 1 month. Thaw before using.

Savoury Horns

Preparation time: 1 hour 30 minutes   Baking time: 20 minutes   Oven setting: 190°C / 375°F   Makes 40

Ingredients

Pastry

Plain (all-purpose) flour	480 g
Baking powder	2 tsp
Pastry margarine	240 g
Butter	75–90 g, at room temperature
Cold water	360–500 ml
Egg yolk	1, beaten
Evaporated milk	2 tsp

Savoury Filling

Cucumber	1, large, peeled, cored and diced
Tomato	1, ripe, blanched, peeled and seeded
Cooked crabmeat or chopped chicken	240 g
Thousand Island dressing	2–3 Tbsp
Ground white pepper	a dash
Salt	a pinch

Method

- Prepare pastry. Sift flour and baking powder into a bowl. Thinly slice pastry margarine into flour with a knife. Either rub in with fingers or blend with a pastry cutter until mixture resembles fine breadcrumbs.

- Mix in butter and cold water. Bind well. Resulting dough should be soft but not too sticky. Cover bowl with a dry cloth. Set aside for 15–30 minutes.

- Preheat oven to 190°C / 375°F.

- Make glaze by beating egg yolk with evaporated milk. Set aside.

- On a floured work surface, roll dough to 1-cm thickness. Fold into thirds. Repeat process of rolling and folding twice. Halve dough for easier handling.

- Roll dough to 2.5-mm thickness. Cut into 30 x 1-cm strips.

- Wind each strip around a cream horn tin, from point to wide end, overlapping slightly. Place on ungreased trays, with exposed end of final round against tray's surface.

- Bake for 20 minutes or until golden. Remove from oven and brush immediately with glaze. Leave to cool before filling.

- Prepare filling. Place crabmeat/chicken, cucumber and tomato into a bowl. Add salad dressing and mix well. Add pepper and salt to taste.

Note:
  Unfilled and unglazed horns keep well in airtight containers for up to 2 weeks.

BREADS

Plaited Apricot Nut Loaf

Preparation time: 2 hours 30 minutes   Baking time: 22–25 minute   Oven setting: 190°C / 375°F   Makes 1

Ingredients

Lukewarm milk	100 ml
Easy blend yeast	6 g
Egg	1, about 75 g, lightly beaten
Bread flour	240 g, sifted
Salt	½ tsp
Unsalted butter	40 g, at room temperature
Hazelnuts	40 g, roughly chopped
Egg white	1, beaten for glazing
Almond flakes	15 g, toasted
Icing sugar for dusting	

Filling

Apricots	75 g, finely diced
Orange juice	100 ml
Rum	1 Tbsp
Sultanas or raisins	30 g

Almond Butter Cream

Unsalted butter	70 g, at room temperature
Brown sugar	40 g
Vanilla essence	1 tsp
Ground almonds	50 g

Method

- Line a large baking tray with greaseproof paper.

- Pour lukewarm milk into a bowl and sprinkle with yeast. Set aside for 3 minutes.

- Place flour, salt and butter into the bowl of an electric mixer fitted with a dough hook. Mix until crumbly.

- Add frothy yeast mixture and beaten egg. Gradually mix into a soft dough. Turn dough out onto a lightly floured work surface. Knead for 5–6 minutes until smooth and elastic. Return to bowl and cover with a damp tea towel. Leave to rise for 1 hour or until doubled in size.

- In the meantime, prepare filling. Place apricots, orange juice and rum in a small saucepan and bring to the boil. Lower heat and simmer for 1 minute. Remove from heat and set aside for 1 hour. Drain apricots and set aside. Place raisins in soaking liquid and leave for 15 minutes. Drain and set aside.

- Prepare almond butter cream. Beat butter, brown sugar and vanilla essence until light and creamy. Stir in ground almonds. Set aside.

- Knock back risen dough using your fists. Turn it out on a lightly floured work surface and roll out into a 30 x 26-cm sheet.

- Spread almond butter cream over dough sheet, then scatter soaked apricots, raisins and chopped hazelnuts evenly over surface. Roll dough up tightly from long side.

- Place roll on prepared tray. Cut roll lengthwise into three equal strips, leaving one end joined. Plait strips, then pinch and tuck in ends. Loosely cover with a damp tea towel and leave for 1 hour or until doubled in size.

- Preheat oven to 190°C / 375°F.

- Bake for 22–25 minutes or until golden brown. Brush immediately with beaten egg white and sprinkle with almond flakes.

- Leave loaf to cool for 15 minutes before removing from tray. Dust with icing sugar if desired. Slice thickly to serve.

Asparagus Mushroom Cheese Loaf

Preparation time: 30 minutes   Baking time: 15 minutes   Oven setting: 175°C / 350°F   Makes 14

Ingredients

Plain (all-purpose) flour	150 g
Baking powder	10 g
Asparagus	200 g, lower ends peeled, cut into 3–4 sections
Fresh shiitake mushrooms	150 g
Butter	60 g
Vegetable oil	1 Tbsp + 100 ml
Shallot	1, peeled and sliced
Spring onion (optional)	30 g, chopped
Large eggs	3, each 70 g
Warm milk	125 ml
Emmental cheese	100 g, grated

Herbs and Seasoning

Dried thyme	½ tsp
Coriander seeds	½ tsp, crushed
Salt	1 tsp
Ground white pepper	½ tsp
Ground black pepper	¼ tsp

Method

- Line a 26.5 x 8-cm loaf pan with greaseproof paper. Preheat oven to 175°C / 350°F.

- Sift flour with baking powder and set aside.

- Blanch asparagus in boiling water. Drain and place in iced water to stop it from over cooking. Chill.

- Remove stems from mushrooms and slice. Set aside.

- Heat butter and 1 Tbsp oil in a saucepan. Lightly brown shallot. Add mushrooms and sauté until starting to soften. Stir in herbs and seasoning. Add spring onion and mix well. Remove from heat and set aside to cool.

- Using an electric mixer, whisk eggs for 2 minutes until light and frothy. Add flour mixture and whisk until just combined and smooth. Add 100 ml oil and warm milk. Whisk until well combined. Add cooled mushroom mixture and cheese. Mix well.

- Pour into prepared pan. Level surface and arranged drained asparagus on surface.

- Bake for 45 minutes or until top is golden brown.

- Leave to cool in pan for 10 minutes before turning out onto a wire rack to cool further.

- Slice and serve with a soup or salad.

Grandma's Pinwheels

Preparation time: 120 minutes   Baking time: 25 minutes   Oven Setting: 175°C / 350°F   Makes 14

Ingredients

Sugar	1 Tbsp
Warm milk	225 ml
Easy blend yeast	10 g
Plain (all-purpose) flour	480 g, sifted
Salt	1 pinch
Lard or corn oil	1 cup
Eggs	4, beaten
Jam	quantity and flavour as desired
Chopped nuts (optional)	130 g
Coarse white sugar	

Method

- Grease baking trays and set aside.

- Dissolve sugar in warm milk. Stir in yeast. Let stand for about 15 minutes until frothy.

- Sift flour into a bowl. Add salt and lard/corn oil. Mix by hand until ingredients well combined. Add beaten eggs. Mix well. Stir in yeast liquid. Beat until smooth. Leave for about 1 hour 30 minutes until dough doubles in volume.

- Preheat oven to 175°C / 350°F.

- Divide dough into two equal portions. On a floured work surface, roll each portion of dough into a 35 x 30-cm rectangle. Spread with jam and top with nuts if desired. Roll up tightly. Using a flour-coated knife, cut each roll into seven slices, each about 2-cm thick.

- Place well apart on greased baking trays. Sprinkle coarse sugar over the top. Bake for 25–30 minutes or until golden brown.

- Leave to cool before serving or storing.

Curry Buns

Preparation time: 1 hour 35 minutes   Baking time: 15 minutes   Oven Setting: 200°C / 400°F   Makes 24

Ingredients

Warm water	225 ml
Milk	225 ml
Sugar	2 Tbsp
Warm milk	225 ml
Easy blend yeast	10 g
Plain (all-purpose) flour	720 g
Salt	1^1/$_2$ tsp
Butter	90 g, at room temperature
Egg yolk	1, beaten
Cooking oil	3–4 drops

Filling

Chicken, beef or pork	240 g, cut into small cubes
Curry powder	2 Tbsp
Cooking oil	2 Tbsp
Onions	2, peeled and diced
Potatoes	2, medium, peeled and cut into small cubes
Salt	1 tsp

Method

- Mix half the warm water with milk. Set aside.

- Dissolve sugar in remaining warm water. Stir in yeast. Let stand for about 15 minutes until frothy.

- Sift flour into a mixing bowl. Add salt. Stir butter into flour. Add diluted milk and yeast liquid. Bind with a wooden spoon.

- On a lightly floured work surface, knead dough until smooth. Return dough to bowl. Cover with a damp tea towel. Leave for about 1 hour 30 minutes or until dough doubles in volume. Punch dough down and let rise again.

- In the meantime, prepare filling. Season meat with curry powder. Set aside. Heat oil in a wok and lightly brown onions. Add potatoes and a little water. Fry until soft. Add seasoned meat and stir-fry until cooked. Add salt and fry until filling is dry. Dish out and leave to cool.

- On a floured work surface, knead dough and form a long roll. Cut into 24 even pieces. Shape into balls, then flatten into rounds.

- Put 1 tsp filling on the centre of each round. Fold in edges and seal. Roll between hands until balls are smooth. Place well apart on greased baking trays. Leave to rise for 10–15 minutes.

- Preheat oven to 200°C / 400°F.

- Bake buns for 15–20 minutes or until golden brown. In the meantime, make glaze by beating egg yolk and oil together.

- Remove buns from oven and immediately brush with glaze.

Crusty Roll

Preparation time: 2 hours   Baking time: 30 minutes   Oven Setting: 200°C / 400°F   Makes 1

Ingredients

Sugar	1 Tbsp
Lukewarm water	225 ml
Easy blend yeast	10 g
Plain (all-purpose) flour	360 g, sifted
Corn oil	$1/2$ Tbsp
Salt	1 tsp
Egg white (A)	1, lightly beaten
Egg white (B)	$1/2$, beaten with 1 Tbsp water

Method

- Dissolve sugar in lukewarm water. Stir in yeast. Let stand for about 15 minutes until frothy.

- Sift half the flour into a mixing bowl. Add corn oil, salt, egg white (A) and yeast liquid. Beat mixture thoroughly. Stir in remaining flour.

- On a floured work surface, knead dough until it is smooth and no longer sticks to hands. Return dough to bowl. Cover with a damp tea towel. Leave for about an hour until dough doubles in volume. Punch dough down and let rise again.

- On a floured work surface, knead then divide dough into three equal portions. Shape each portion into a 30-cm long roll.

- Plait (braid) three rolls together. Secure at both ends. Place on a greased baking tray. Brush with water. Let rise until double in volume.

- Preheat oven to 200°C / 400°F.

- Just before putting loaf in the oven, place a pan half-filled with boiling water on oven's bottom shelf. Bake for 15 minutes then lower temperature to 175°C / 350°F and bake for a further 12 minutes or until loaf is golden brown.

- About 5 minutes before removing from oven, brush loaf with glaze.

- Remove from oven. Leave to cool on a wire rack before serving or storing.

Note:

To make baguettes using this recipe, divide dough into two portions instead of three. Form each portion into a long roll. Brush with water, then cut diagonal slits across the top with a sharp knife.

Pizza

Preparation time: 2 hours   Cooking time: 15 minutes   Baking time: 20 minutes   Oven Setting: 200°C / 400°F   Makes 1

Ingredients

Sugar	$^1/_2$ Tbsp
Water	115 ml, lukewarm
Easy blend yeast	8 g
Plain (all-purpose) flour	240 g
Salt	1 pinch
Corn oil	2 tsp
Grated cheese	as desired

Tomato Sauce

Tomatoes	360 g, ripe
Beef or pork	180 g, minced
Sugar	$^1/_2$ tsp
Ground black pepper	a dash
Salt	$^1/_2$ tsp
Cooking oil	1 Tbsp
Garlic	3 cloves, peeled and minced
Shallots	3, sliced
Tomato purée	4 tsp

Method

- Dissolve sugar in water. Stir in yeast. Let stand for 15 minutes until liquid frothy.

- Sift flour into a mixing bowl. Add salt and corn oil. Blend with a pastry cutter. Add yeast liquid. Mix with a wooden spoon.

- On a lightly floured work surface, knead dough until smooth. Return dough to bowl. Cover with damp tea towel. Leave until dough doubles in volume. Punch dough down and let rise again.

- Prepare tomato sauce. Soak tomatoes in boiling water for 5 minutes or until skins become loose or split. Transfer to a bowl of cold water and peel off skins. Roughly chop peeled tomatoes and set aside. Season meat with sugar, pepper and salt. Heat oil in a wok and lightly brown garlic and shallots. Add seasoned meat and stir-fry for a few minutes before dishing out. Add tomatoes to wok. Simmer gently until quite dry. Add tomato purée and cooked meat. Adjust to taste with pepper, salt and sugar. Dish out and set aside to cool.

- On a floured work surface, roll risen dough to fit a well-greased 27.5 x 17.5-cm baking tray. Leave to rise for 10–15 minutes.

- Preheat oven to 200°C / 400°F.

- Spread tomato sauce on dough. Top with cheese. Bake for 20–25 minutes or until crust is golden brown. Slice to serve.

SAVOURIES

Siew Mai

Preparation time: 1 hour 30 minutes   Cooking time: 12 minutes   Makes 40

Ingredients

Wonton skins (7.5-cm squares)	150 g
Cooked crab roe	1 Tbsp

Filling

Peeled prawns (shrimps)	240 g, deveined and minced
Fatty minced pork	240 g
Cooked crabmeat	120 g
Salt	1 tsp
Sesame oil	$^1/_2$ tsp
Ground white pepper	a dash
Egg white	1
Cornflour	$1^1/_2$ Tbsp
Corn oil	1 Tbsp
Dried Chinese mushrooms	2, soaked, stems discarded and minced
Water chestnuts	3, peeled and chopped
Spring onion (scallion)	1 stalk, thinly sliced

Method

- Prepare filling. Combine prawns, pork and crabmeat. Season with salt, sesame oil, pepper and egg white. Stir in cornflour and corn oil. Beat mixture with a spoon. Mix in mushrooms, water chestnuts and spring onion. Refrigerate for 1 hour.

- Using a 7.5-cm round cutter, cut wonton skins into rounds.

- To form *siew mai*, place 2 tsp filling on each round. Gather edges of skin and smooth it upwards around filling. Pleating will occur naturally.

- Place *siew mai* in lined or greased bamboo baskets. Place a little crab roe on top of each dumpling. Steam for 12 minutes.

Note:
  If crab roe is unavailable, mix 1 Tbsp filling with 2 drops orange food colouring and use as decorative topping.

Fried Wontons

Preparation time: 45 minutes   Cooking time: 15 minutes   Makes 60

Ingredients

Wonton skins (7.5-cm squares)	150 g
Egg white	1, beaten
Cooking oil for deep-frying	

Filling

Small–medium prawns (shrimps)	120 g
Egg white	$1/2$
Light soy sauce	1 tsp
Sugar	$1/2$ tsp
Salt	a pinch
Ground white pepper	a dash
Spring onion (scallion)	1, finely sliced
Coriander (cilantro) leaves	1 sprig, chopped

Method

- Prepare filling. Peel and rinse prawns. Pat-dry and cut each prawn into 2–3 pieces. Season with egg white, light soy sauce, sugar, salt and pepper. Set aside for at least 30 minutes. Mix in spring onion and coriander just before using.

- To form wontons, place a wonton skin on a working surface with one corner pointing at you.

- Place a few pieces of prawn near the bottom corner of the wonton skin. Fold the lowest tip over prawns to meet the centre of the skin.

- From the folded edge, roll up until just past the widest part of the square.

- Lift both ends of rolled section, position above filling, and stick together using beaten egg white.

- Heat oil in a wok over medium heat. Gently lower wontons into hot oil. Deep-fry in small batches until golden. Drain well.

- Serve hot with chilli sauce on the side.

Steamed Char Siew Buns

Preparation time: 2 hours 30 minutes   Cooking time: 30 minutes   Makes 32

Ingredients

Dough

Sugar	115 g
Warm water	340 ml
Easy blend yeast	15 g
Plain (all-purpose) flour	675 g
Baking powder	$^1/_2$ Tbsp
Bicarbonate of soda	$^1/_3$ tsp
Salt	1 tsp
Corn oil	1 Tbsp

Filling

Streaky pork or skinless chicken	600 g
Salt	2 tsp
Sugar	3 Tbsp
Light soy sauce	1 Tbsp
Dark soy sauce	$^1/_2$ tsp
Red food colouring	a few drops
Water	450 ml
Oyster sauce	2 tsp
Sesame oil	$^1/_2$ tsp
Cornflour	2 tsp
Coriander (cilantro) leaves	1 sprig, chopped

Method

- Prepare filling. Rinse meat and pat dry with paper towels. Cut into 2.5-cm strips. Season with salt, sugar and soy sauces. Add food colouring and mix well. Cover and refrigerate for at least 2 hours or overnight.

- Place meat on a wire mesh on a roasting tray. Grill in the oven with a pan of water on the bottom shelf. Turn pieces occasionally until cooked through. Remove meat from mesh and reserve gravy. Set aside to cool before dicing.

- Place 4 Tbsp gravy, oyster sauce, sesame oil and cornflour in a wok. Bring to the boil. Stir in diced meat and coriander. Mix well. Dish out and set aside to cool.

- Prepare dough. Dissolve sugar in water. Stir in yeast. Let stand for 10–15 minutes until frothy.

- Sift flour, baking powder and bicarbonate of soda into a bowl. Add salt and mix. Gradually add corn oil and yeast liquid, stirring with a wooden spoon. When mixture becomes too difficult to stir, use hands to form a firm dough.

- On a lightly floured work surface, knead dough for at least 10 minutes. Sprinkle with flour occasionally to prevent dough from sticking to the work surface.

- Return dough to bowl. Cover with a damp tea towel and leave for about 1 hour 30 minutes until dough doubles in volume. Punch dough down and let rise again for 20–30 minutes.

- On a lightly floured work surface, knead dough until smooth. Form two rolls, each 4 cm in diameter, then cut into 2-cm thick pieces. You should get about 32 pieces altogether. Flatten each round with a rolling pin.

- Place 1 tsp filling on the centre of each dough circle. To seal, lift one edge of dough and form pleats in one direction. Twist pleats together at the top to secure.

- Place buns on squares of greaseproof paper. Arrange well apart in bamboo baskets. Steam over high heat for 12 minutes.

- Serve immediately.

Steamed Flower Buns

Preparation time: 2 hours 30 minutes   Cooking time: 12 minutes   Makes 14

Ingredients

Sugar	2 Tbsp
Warm water	3 Tbsp
Easy blend yeast	10 g
Plain (all-purpose) flour	450 g
Baking powder	1 tsp
Bicarbonate of soda	$1/3$ tsp
Salt	1 tsp
Milk	180 ml, mixed with 4 Tbsp water
Corn oil	

Method

- Dissolve sugar in water. Stir in yeast. Let stand for 10–15 minutes until frothy.

- Sift flour, baking powder and bicarbonate of soda into a bowl. Add salt. Gradually add milk and yeast liquid, stirring with a wooden spoon. When dough becomes too difficult to stir, use hands to form a firm dough.

- On a floured work surface, knead dough for 10 minutes or until smooth. Return dough to bowl. Cover with a damp tea towel. Leave for 1 hour 30 minutes until dough doubles in volume. Punch dough down and let rise again for 20–30 minutes.

- On a floured work surface, knead dough for 5 minutes or until smooth. Divide dough into 2 parts. Roll each portion into a 30 x 12.5-cm rectangle. Brush with corn oil. Carefully roll up lengthways. Cut into 2.5-cm thick rounds.

- Stack two pieces to form a standing figure 8, with swirls facing you. With a flour-coated chopstick, press down lengthways, or parallel to swirls, along centre of top edge. To secure the joining of two pieces, pinch them together at both ends of chopstick-marked line.

- Place buns on squares of greaseproof paper. Arrange well apart in bamboo baskets. Steam over high heat for 12 minutes.

- Serve immediately.

Prawn Balls

Preparation time: 1 hour   Cooking time: 15 minutes   Makes 50

Ingredients

Small–medium prawns (shrimps)	600 g
Light soy sauce	2 tsp
Sesame oil	1 tsp
Salt	$^1/_2$ tsp
Sugar	$^1/_2$ tsp
Ground white pepper	a dash
Egg white	$^1/_2$
Cornflour	1 tsp
Spring onions (scallions)	2 stalks, finely sliced
Coriander (cilantro) leaves	1 sprig, finely sliced
Water chestnuts	4, peeled and minced
Day-old sliced bread	600 g, cut into very small cubes
Cooking oil for deep-frying	

Chilli Sauce

Red chillies	12, large and seeded
Garlic	3 cloves, peeled
Water	225 ml
Tomato sauce	2 Tbsp
Vinegar	$^1/_2$ Tbsp
Sugar	$^1/_2$ Tbsp
Salt	$^1/_4$ tsp
Cooking oil	1 Tbsp

Method

- Prepare chilli sauce. Blend chillies and garlic with water into a fine paste. Transfer to a small saucepan. Add remaining ingredients and bring to the boil. Cook for a few miunutes, then remove from heat and set aside to cool completely. Store in airtight jars at room temperature.

- Peel and rinse prawns. Pat-dry with paper towels. Mince to a fine paste.

- Season minced prawns with soy sauce, sesame oil, salt, sugar, pepper, egg white and cornflour. Stir in spring onions, coriander and water chestnuts. Refrigerate for at least 30 minutes.

- Drop teaspoonfuls of mixture onto bread cubes and form bread-coated balls. You should get about 50 pieces.

- Heat oil for deep-frying over low heat. Gently lower balls into hot oil and cook in small batches until golden. Drain well.

- Serve prawns balls with chilli sauce on the side.

Kuih Pie Tee

Preparation time: 1 hour   Cooking time: 1 hour 30 m minutes   Makes 38–40

Ingredients

Pie tee shells

Plain (all-purpose) flour	90 g
Rice flour	1 Tbsp
Salt	$^1/_4$ tsp
Egg	1, beaten
Water	170 ml
Cooking oil for deep-frying	

Filling

Cooking oil	3 Tbsp
Garlic	4 cloves, peeled and minced
Turnip	450 g, peeled, finely shredded and squeezed of excess water
Chicken or pork	240 g, diced
Peeled prawns (shrimps)	240 g, diced
Salt	1 tsp
Ground white pepper	$^1/_4$ tsp
Five-spice powder	$^1/_4$ tsp
Crabmeat	90 g
Chinese lettuce	a bunch
Crisp-fried shallots	1 Tbsp
Coriander (cilantro) leaves	1 sprig, chopped

Method

- Prepare *pie tee* shells. Sift flours into a small bowl. Add salt. Stir in egg. Mix with water to achieve a smooth, runny batter. Strain batter if lumpy.

- Heat oil in a deep pan. Warm *pie tee* iron in hot oil for 1 minute.

- Dip hot iron in batter, then place into hot oil. Fry until shell is golden before loosening from iron. Cook for a few more seconds before removing from hot oil. Drain well.

- Let shells cool completely before storing in airtight containers until needed.

- Prepare filling. Heat oil in a wok and lightly brown garlic. Add turnip and stir-fry until tender. Add chicken or pork and prawns. Season with salt, pepper and five-spice powder. Stir in crabmeat. Simmer until quite dry. Dish out and leave to cool.

- To assemble, line a *pie tee* shell with small pieces of lettuce. Add 2 tsp filling. Garnish with crisp-fried shallots and coriander leaves. Serve with your favourite chilli sauce.

Roti Jala with Chicken Curry

Preparation time: 30 minutes   Cooking time: 30 minutes   Makes 20–24

Ingredients

Roti Jala

Plain (all-purpose) flour	240 g
Salt	$^1/_2$ tsp
Eggs	2, beaten
Coconut milk	565 ml, squeezed from $^1/_2$ grated coconut and sufficient water
Cooking oil	as needed

Chicken Curry

Shallots	250 g, peeled and chopped
Candlenuts (buah keras)	5–6
Lemon grass (serai)	1 stalk
Dried chillies	10, soaked
Chicken curry powder	5 Tbsp
Salt	1 tsp and more to taste
Cooking oil	55 ml
Coconut cream	250 ml, squeezed from 1 grated coconut and sufficient water
Coconut milk	1.25 litres, squeezed from same grated coconut and sufficient water
Chicken	1.5 kg, cut into bite-size pieces

Method

- Prepare curry. Blend shallots, candlenuts, lemon grass and chillies together. Mix with curry powder and 1 tsp salt.

- Heat oil in a wok. Fry curry powder mixture until fragrant. Add 2 Tbsp coconut cream to prevent drying. Add chicken and fry for a few minutes with 2–3 Tbsp coconut milk to prevent ingredients from sticking to the wok.

- Add remaining coconut milk. Simmer until chicken is tender. Add remaining coconut cream. Adjust to taste with salt. Keep warm while preparing *roti jala*.

- Prepare *roti jala*. Sift flour into a bowl. Add salt. Stir in eggs and coconut milk. Beat until smooth. Strain batter if lumpy.

- Grease a nonstick pan. Place over low heat. Position *roti jala* cup over pan. Add a ladleful of batter, then move cup in a circular motion over pan to create a lacy pancake. Cook until batter changes colour. Transfer to a dish. Repeat until batter is used up. You should get 20–24 pancakes.

- When cool, fold pancakes in eighths or fold and roll up. Serve with a chicken curry.

Savoury Pancakes

Preparation time: 30 minutes   Cooking time: 30 minutes   Makes 12

Ingredients

Cooking oil	3 Tbsp
Shallots	3, peeled and sliced
Dried prawns (shrimps)	75 g, soaked and minced
Plain (all-purpose) flour	300 g
Water	450 ml
Salt	$^1/_4$ tsp
Ground white pepper	$^1/_4$ tsp
Spring onions (scallions)	2–3, finely sliced
Chilli sauce	to taste

Method

- Heat oil in a nonstick pan. Fry shallots until lightly browned. Drain and set aside.

- Add dried prawns to wok. Fry over low heat until fragrant and crisp. Drain and set aside. Remove oil and reserve for frying pancakes later.

- Sift flour into a bowl. Stir in water to make a smooth, runny batter. Strain batter if lumpy. Stir in salt, pepper and spring onions. Mix in crisp-fried shallots and dried prawns.

- Lightly grease nonstick pan. Add a ladleful of batter. Fry both sides until lightly brown.

- Roll pancakes up and serve with chilli sauce.

Puri

Preparation time: 30 minutes   Cooking time: 30 minutes   Makes 24

Ingredients

Wholemeal (*atta*) flour	240 g
Plain (all-purpose) flour	120 g
Semolina	60 g
Salt	1 tsp
Corn oil	4 tsp
Cooking oil for deep-frying	

Method

• Sift flours and semolina into a bowl. Add salt and corn oil. Knead into a firm dough with a little water.

• Shape dough into 24 small balls. On a floured work surface, flatten balls into thin rounds with a rolling pin.

• Heat oil for deep-frying over medium heat. Lower puri into hot oil in batches and deep-fry until puri is inflated and lightly browned.

• Drain well. Serve hot with chicken curry (page 138).

Weights & Measures

Quantities for this book are given in Metric and American (spoon and cup) measures. Standard spoon and cup measurements used are: 1 teaspoon = 5 ml, 1 tablespoon = 15 ml, 1 cup = 250 ml. All measures are level unless otherwise stated.

LIQUID AND VOLUME MEASURES

Metric	Imperial	American
5 ml	$1/6$ fl oz	1 teaspoon
10 ml	$1/3$ fl oz	1 dessertspoon
15 ml	$1/2$ fl oz	1 tablespoon
60 ml	2 fl oz	$1/4$ cup (4 tablespoons)
85 ml	$2^{1}/2$ fl oz	$1/3$ cup
90 ml	3 fl oz	$3/8$ cup (6 tablespoons)
125 ml	4 fl oz	$1/2$ cup
180 ml	6 fl oz	$3/4$ cup
250 ml	8 fl oz	1 cup
300 ml	10 fl oz ($1/2$ pint)	$1^{1}/4$ cups
375 ml	12 fl oz	$1^{1}/2$ cups
435 ml	14 fl oz	$1^{3}/4$ cups
500 ml	16 fl oz	2 cups
625 ml	20 fl oz (1 pint)	$2^{1}/2$ cups
750 ml	24 fl oz ($1^{1}/5$ pints)	3 cups
1 litre	32 fl oz ($1^{3}/5$ pints)	4 cups
1.25 litres	40 fl oz (2 pints)	5 cups
1.5 litres	48 fl oz ($2^{2}/5$ pints)	6 cups
2.5 litres	80 fl oz (4 pints)	10 cups

DRY MEASURES

Metric	Imperial
30 grams	1 ounce
45 grams	$1^{1}/2$ ounces
55 grams	2 ounces
70 grams	$2^{1}/2$ ounces
85 grams	3 ounces
100 grams	$3^{1}/2$ ounces
110 grams	4 ounces
125 grams	$4^{1}/2$ ounces
140 grams	5 ounces
280 grams	10 ounces
450 grams	16 ounces (1 pound)
500 grams	1 pound, $1^{1}/2$ ounces
700 grams	$1^{1}/2$ pounds
800 grams	$1^{3}/4$ pounds
1 kilogram	2 pounds, 3 ounces
1.5 kilograms	3 pounds, $4^{1}/2$ ounces
2 kilograms	4 pounds, 6 ounces

LENGTH

Metric	Imperial
0.5 cm	$1/4$ inch
1 cm	$1/2$ inch
1.5 cm	$3/4$ inch
2.5 cm	1 inch

OVEN TEMPERATURE

	°C	°F	Gas Regulo
Very slow	120	250	1
Slow	150	300	2
Moderately slow	160	325	3
Moderate	180	350	4
Moderately hot	190/200	370/400	5/6
Hot	210/220	410/440	6/7
Very hot	230	450	8
Super hot	250/290	475/550	9/10

ABBREVIATION

Tbsp	tablespoon
tsp	teaspoon
kg	kilogram
g	gram
l	litres
ml	millilitre